20TH CENTURY ART
1960-80
EXPERIMENTS *and* NEW DIRECTION

Please visit our web site at: www.garethstevens.com
For a free color catalog describing Gareth Stevens' list of high-quality books
and multimedia programs, call 1-800-542-2595 (USA) or 1-800-461-9120 (Canada).
Gareth Stevens Publishing's Fax: (414) 332-3567.

Library of Congress Cataloging-in-Publication Data available upon request from publisher.
Fax (414) 336-0157 for the attention of the Publishing Records Department.

ISBN 0-8368-2852-6

This North American edition first published in 2001 by
Gareth Stevens Publishing
A World Almanac Education Group Company
330 West Olive Street, Suite 100
Milwaukee, WI 53212 USA

Original edition © 2000 by David West Children's Books. First published in Great Britain in 2000 by
Heinemann Library, Halley Court, Jordan Hill, Oxford OX2 8EJ, a division of Reed Educational and
Professional Publishing Limited. This U.S. edition © 2001 by Gareth Stevens, Inc. Additional end
matter © 2001 by Gareth Stevens, Inc.

Picture Research: Brooks Krikler Research
Picture Editor: Carlotta Cooper
Gareth Stevens Editor: Valerie J. Weber

Photo Credits:
Abbreviations: (t) top, (m) middle, (b) bottom, (l) left, (r) right

AKG London: pages 7, 15(t).
AKG London © Apple Records: pages 5(t), 13(t).
AKG London/Private Collection: page 29(l).
Bridgeman Art Library: pages 18(t), 25, 29(r).
Bridgeman Art Library © ADAGP, Paris, and DACS, London, 2000: pages 6(t), 9(t).
Bridgeman Art Library © The Andy Warhol Foundation for the Visual Arts Inc./ARS, New York,
    and DACS, London, 2000: page 11(t).
Bridgeman Art Library © ARS, New York, and DACS, London, 2000: page 15(b).
Bridgeman Art Library/Bradford Art Galleries: cover, pages 12(br), 13(bl).
Bridgeman Art Library/Private Collection: page 24(b).
Christie's Images © DACS 2000: page 16(b).
Corbally Stourton Contemporary Art/Bridgeman Art Library: page 26(l).
Corbis/Page: pages 3, 21(t).
Corbis © Succession Marcel Duchamp/ADAGP, Paris, and DACS, London, 2000: page 17(b).
Courtesy XXO Mobilier et Design, Paris: page 10(r).
Caroline Graville/Redferns: page 12(bl).
Hulton Getty Collection: pages 4(both), 5(b), 6(b), 8(both), 9(b), 10(l), 11(m, b), 12(t), 13(br), 16(t),
    18(b), 19(t), 20(both), 21(b), 23(both), 24(t), 26(r), 27, 28(both).
Reproduced by kind permission of Gilbert & George, with thanks to the Anthony d'Offay Gallery:
    page 19(b).
Tate Gallery © Carl Andre/VAGA, New York/DACS, London, 2000: page 22.

Printed in the United States of America

1 2 3 4 5 6 7 8 9 05 04 03 02 01

20TH CENTURY ART
1960-80

EXPERIMENTS and NEW DIRECTION

Clare Oliver

Gareth Stevens Publishing
A WORLD ALMANAC EDUCATION GROUP COMPANY

CONTENTS

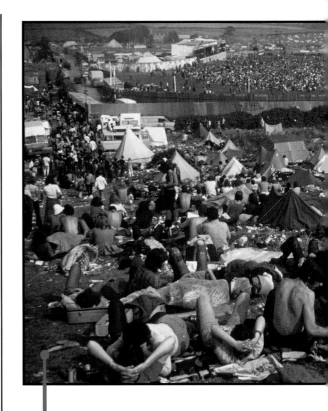

1960s music, youth culture, radical politics — the 1969 Woodstock Music and Art Fair came to symbolize them all. Half a million fans flocked to camp in a meadow and groove to the best rock music of the decade.

No longer restricted to the gallery, art hit the fashion world. These dresses show the dazzling influence of Op Art.

REVOLUTIONS IN ART

The 1960s and 1970s were a time for bold experiments in all aspects of culture. It is impossible to pinpoint a single dominant art style — art was exploding in every direction.

The period began with artists shedding the influence of the Abstract Expressionists. Pop artists moved away from emotion to pictures and sculptures of new goods that it seemed everyone could buy. Later, the Superrealists continued the Pop emphasis on images of popular culture with their paintings that looked like photos and sculptures that looked like real people.

Abstract art really came into its own during the 1960s and 1970s — from Op Art to the Minimalists. Conceptualism was the most avant-garde of all the art movements. Conceptual artists used language, their own bodies, theatrical stunts, performances, or even the environment to create startling works that made the viewer have a fresh look at the world.

5

Youth culture pulsed to the beat of popular music, and the Beatles led the way in shifting styles. British Pop artist Peter Blake (b. 1932) and his wife designed the album cover for their Sgt. Peppers Lonely Hearts Club Band.

Roy Lichtenstein, 1963
Pop artist Roy Lichtenstein (1923–1997) borrowed from everyday culture with his huge, comic-strip canvases.

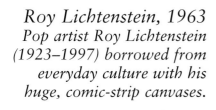

MOVE IT!

Early-20th-century Russian Constructivists had added a fourth dimension — movement — to sculpture by using machinery in their work. Moving sculpture popped up next in the United States in the 1930s, when Alexander Calder (1898–1976) began to build wind-powered mobiles.

THE POWER TO MOVE

Calder developed Kinetic Art, or moving sculpture (from the Greek word *kinesis*). Motors powered some of his early pieces, but Calder usually relied on a wind to move his art. Wind power introduced an element of chance, since the movement of the mobile was unpredictable. Swiss artist Jean Tinguely (1925–1991) used scrapped, old machinery to power his sculptures, which were often designed to self-destruct.

6

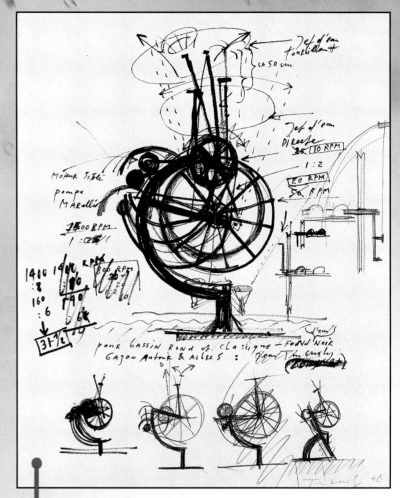

AU BASSIN ROND ET CLASSIQUE, *Jean Tinguely, 1969*

Tinguely collected the parts for his sculpture from a garbage dump. After selecting the parts, he drew plans of how they would fit together into a moving sculpture before building the piece.

ICE SCULPTURES

Why go to all the trouble of making art that won't last or will destroy itself? For many people, the short life span of the artwork makes the experience of it even more beautiful. Each short-lived piece is unique and cannot be exactly duplicated. Ice sculptures are an ideal example of short-lived art. In Ottawa, Canada, ice sculptures are displayed for the Winterlude Festival each February. Each sculpture may take more than a week of full-time work to create.

Huge ice sculptures soon melt in the winter sun.

MODELS FOR *RED, BLUE, AND BLACK*
ALEXANDER CALDER, 1967

This photograph was taken of Calder working on models for the huge, 46-foot- (14-meter-) wide motorized mobile called *Red, Blue, and Black* in his studio. Calder once said that he wished to make "moving Mondrians." Like Piet Mondrian (1872-1944), he used black, white, and primary colors and worked with abstract shapes. *Red, Blue, and Black* was installed in the Dallas Airport. Kinetic sculpture was a popular choice for public spaces. Its movement amused people while they were waiting.

A TRIBUTE TO NEW YORK

One of Tinguely's most famous pieces was *Homage to New York*. The artist assembled pieces of junk in front of New York's Museum of Modern Art. The sculpture had all sorts of odd parts — pieces of piano, bicycle wheels and horns, a weather balloon, and vials of smoke — and was designed to self-destruct. *Homage* did not work as planned. It burst into flames and the fire department had to be called! However, Tinguely was delighted with its spluttering performance. He wanted to make fun of people's blind faith in technology by showing how quickly objects became silly and useless.

MOVERS AND BREAKERS

The name Auto-destructive Art came from its German-born pioneer, Gustav Metzger (*b.* 1926). For one of his pieces, performed in London in 1961, Metzger spray painted acid onto nylon. The acid burned beautiful patterns into the fabric but also destroyed the whole piece! Metzger did not like the way the art market reduced artworks to being primarily about money. A piece that self-destructed provided the viewer with an experience but could not be sold — and escaped the workings of the art market.

OP ART

Some art creates the illusion of movement even though it doesn't actually move. This is known as Op Art, which is short for Optical Art. *Time Magazine* coined the term in 1964, and the next year, the Museum of Modern Art in New York held the first Op Art exhibition.

Riley said that artists should be "workmanlike" in their approach. She uses studio assistants to paint her large designs.

POWERS OF PERCEPTION

This exhibition, called "The Responsive Eye," featured works by British artist Bridget Riley (*b*. 1931). Until about 1966, Riley used only black and white. Pieces such as *Blaze I* (1962), *Fall* (1963), and *Descending* (1965) seem to spin, vibrate, or move. When Riley started using color, she chose candy-colored stripes, working with bold, bright hues that seemed to make each stripe swirl and turn.

COLOR THEORY

Richard Anuszkiewicz (*b*. 1930) was the leading Op artist in the United States. He had studied under Josef Albers (1888–1976), who created a series of paintings called *Homage to the Square* (1949–1976) that explored the effects of different color combinations. Albers placed smaller squares inside larger ones. Depending on the colors used, the shapes might seem to move or switch. Anuszkiewicz continued his teacher's work, using colored lines that seemed to glow out.

Op Art's geometric style captured the spirit of the time. Optical patterns were everywhere! In 1965, Riley sued a U.S. clothing firm for stealing her designs. At the 1968 Olympics, Op Art's influence could be seen in everything from the logo to the pavilions.

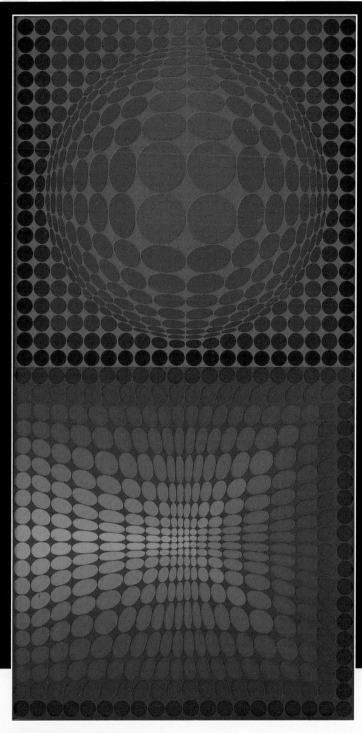

2170VP/106
VICTOR VASARELY, 1969

Hungarian-French artist Victor Vasarely (1908–1997) was the father of Op Art. During the 1930s, Vasarely worked as a poster designer in Paris. After the late 1940s, his paintings featured the same visual tricks that he had used in his advertising work. Using geometrical forms, he tried to create the illusion of three-dimensional objects.

This piece shows how Vasarely applied simple rules to make the image appear to bulge forward or sink inward. One visual rule is that objects that are farther away look smaller. Vasarely used this rule to create the projecting globe at the top of the canvas. By making the spot pattern on the circle get smaller around the edges and also appear to bend, he turns it from a two-dimensional circle into a three-dimensional sphere. On the bottom half of this canvas, Vasarely does the opposite, creating the illusion of a hollow or indent by designing the pattern so that it distorts and shrinks as it moves toward the center.

Vasarely thought that the artist was just an artisan, practicing a trade or skill. Maybe that's why he gave this piece a serial number instead of a title.

OP ART BUILDING
During the 1960s, Vasarely lived and worked in southern France. He believed that artists should produce many works so their art could be available to ordinary people, not just to wealthy people. He set up the Vasarely Foundation to display his work to the public and designed the building himself. The structure is a series of cubes. With their alternate black-and-white circles, they are a giant example of Op Art.

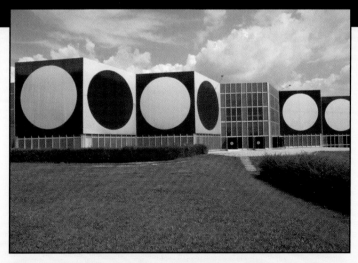

The Vasarely Foundation at Aix-en-Provence, France

AMERICAN POP ART

Ask anyone to name an art movement of the 1960s, and they'll probably say Pop Art. It had instant appeal. In the United States, it was a reaction against the highly charged (but exhausting) emotion favored by the Abstract Expressionists.

FROM INSIDE TO OUT

A famous Abstract Expressionist, Jackson Pollock (1912–1956) painted to express his deepest emotions. When fellow-American Jasper Johns (*b.* 1930) began experimenting with everyday items instead of inner feelings, the method of copying those items became the art.

CAMPBELL'S SOUP CANS
ANDY WARHOL, 1965

In Andy Warhol's early paintings, images of famous brands, such as Coca-Cola, Campbell's soup, and Brillo pads, were repeated on a grid. They looked as if they were on supermarket shelves. After 1962, Warhol stopped painting these images and began silk-screening them instead. This mimicked how consumer goods were mass-produced. It was also a way to eliminate the artist. Even so, Warhol *is* present — in the way he composes his grids of images and in his use of a rainbow of colors.

President John F. Kennedy and wife, Jackie, the day he was shot in 1963

10

TRAGIC ICONS
The glamorous people that Warhol chose to paint revealed the tragic side of fame. One of his subjects was Marilyn Monroe, the famous actress who died of a drug overdose in 1962. Another was First Lady Jackie Kennedy, whose husband was assassinated in Dallas, Texas.

COOL STUFF

In the United States, the key Pop figures were Roy Lichtenstein, Andy Warhol (1928–1987), and Swedish-born sculptor Claes Oldenburg (*b.* 1929). Warhol said Pop was about creating "images that anyone . . . could recognize in a split second . . . all the great modern things that the Abstract Expressionists had tried not to notice." This meant comics, movie stars, junk food, and packaging — all the stuff of consumer culture. Oldenburg even called his studio "The Store," filling it with plaster models of food or soft sculptures.

Jonathan Da Pas's Joe *chair (1970) paid tribute to popular baseball star Joe Di Maggio. The soft sculptures made by Oldenburg — giant, squishy models of familiar objects such as hamburgers or sundaes — inspired the design.*

EVERYDAY OBJECTS BECOME ART

Using everyday objects as art shifted the viewer's attention from the object itself to the surface of the art and the artist's methods. Images used in Pop art were taken out of their usual surroundings. Sometimes the images were enlarged, as in Lichtenstein's comic strips, or painted in different colors, as in Warhol's work. This forced the viewer to concentrate on form and composition, not on the objects. Lichtenstein said about his comic strips that "half the time they are upside down anyway when I work."

Assistants made Warhol's prints in his studio, called "The Factory," but he often added extra color with a brush.

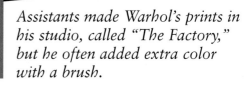

Many of Lichtenstein's works, such as Whaam! *(1963), were blown up from romance or war comics. Lichtenstein supplied just one or two frames of the story so the images were out of their normal setting. The real subject matter was the way the art was made – the flat color, the thick black outlines, and the precise representation of colored dots.*

BRITISH POP

The British brand of Pop Art was born in the 1950s when Richard Hamilton (*b.* 1922) created his 1956 Pop collage *Just What Is It That Makes Today's Homes So Different, So Appealing?* This work celebrated and criticized Americans' urge to constantly buy, hoping to gain happiness from their possessions.

GRADUATION DAY

Pop Art exploded with the "Young Contemporaries" exhibition (1961). The artists were recent graduates of Great Britain's Royal College of Art — David Hockney (*b.* 1937), R. B. Kitaj (*b.* 1932), Allen Jones (*b.* 1937), and Derek Boshier (*b.* 1937). Hockney was an instant celebrity and became a major success.

Ossie Clark at work in 1969

FASHION GURU

One of Hockney's most famous portraits was *Mr. and Mrs. Clark and Percy* (1970–1971). It showed top fashion designer Ossie Clark (1942–1996), his wife, and pet cat. As in many of Hockney's pictures of friends, simple details suggested a modern, wealthy lifestyle.

12

Baby boomers born after World War II became a huge new youth market. Eager consumers of fashion, art, and pop, they created their own unique styles.

WHAT IS POP?

Richard Hamilton created a famous list of the qualities of Pop in 1957. It was to be "popular, transient, expendable, low-cost, mass-produced, young, witty, sexy, gimmicky, glamorous, and Big Business."

It was the Swinging Sixties. Britain was at the head of a cultural revolution in the fields of pop, film, photography, and fashion.

POP FROM THE PAST

Pop artist Peter Blake (*b.* 1932) loved nostalgia, as seen in his design for the Beatles' album, *Sgt. Pepper's Lonely Hearts Club Band.* Working in collage, he used popular objects, such as toys, magazine photos, and movie tickets. Blake depicted the pinups of the past, such as wrestlers and boxers, as well as the pop and movie stars of the day.

SGT. PEPPER'S LONELY HEARTS CLUB BAND, *Peter Blake and Jann Haworth, 1967*

Blake first painted the Beatles in 1962 and designed their 1967 album with his wife, who made several of the stuffed figures.

13

THE DIVER
DAVID HOCKNEY, 1971

In 1963, Hockney visited Los Angeles, attracted by its easy living. His paintings of the city celebrate hot sunshine, blue pools, tall palms, and modern buildings. Hockney's style was simple, but his desire to represent shadows, ripples, or splashes led him to try out different media. For *The Diver,* he used pressed paper pulp.

Hockney (right) moved to California in 1976.

ART AS IDEA

In 1917, Marcel Duchamp (1887–1968) displayed a urinal, called it *Fountain,* and presented it as art. This act gave birth to Conceptualism, the theory that the idea or concept behind the art could be more important than the actual piece.

THE IDEA OF ART

In 1967, U.S. artist Sol LeWitt (*b.* 1928) wrote, "In Conceptual Art, the idea or concept is . . . most important. . . . The idea becomes the machine that makes the art." One problem explored in Conceptual Art is expressing meaning. Many '60s and '70s artists used words to do this, including Americans Robert Rauschenberg (*b.* 1925), Robert Barry (*b.* 1936), and Joseph Kosuth (*b.* 1945) and Art & Language, a group of English artists founded in the late 1960s.

This is the logo for Biba, a famous fashion store in London. In posters and ads, words and images mix to create a new meaning that signifies the brand.

LANGUAGE AND STRUCTURALISM

Joseph Kosuth's early interest in dictionary definitions soon expanded to include the meanings in academic texts and literature. Artists were particularly intrigued by meaning during the 1960s and 1970s after a movement known as Structuralism had arisen in France. The Structuralists were concerned with meaning. Although they primarily focused on literature, they wanted to know and show how anything — from a bus ticket to a novel, an advertisement to a work of art — conveys its meaning. They tried to identify a set of rules that would explain methods of communication. They based their work on the studies of signs and symbols made by the Swiss scholar Ferdinand de Saussure (1857–1913). French Structuralist Roland Barthes (1915–1980) believed that a novel or a work of art was simply a system of signs and that viewers created the meaning for themselves. This annoyed some people because it meant the author or artist was no longer responsible for creating meaning.

DEFINING ART

Kosuth went further than most artists in using language as both the material and the subject of his art. His piece *One and Three Chairs* (1965) displayed a real chair, a same-sized photograph of it, and a definition of *chair.* Kosuth disturbs viewers by presenting several different realities, questioning the way they define things — which reality represents a chair the best?

THIS IS A PORTRAIT OF IRIS CLERT IF I SAY SO

If a urinal could be art because the artist said so, then so could anything! Rauschenberg's piece for a Parisian exhibition in 1960 was a telegram with these words (left).

14

ALL KINDS OF MEANING

Dictionary definitions are supposed to be as precise as possible. In the same way, an artist might try to simplify an idea so that its meaning is clear to the viewer. However, many of the language pieces prove how impossible this is. Words have many meanings, and even the artist can't predict how a viewer will respond. For example, in *It is . . . Inconsistent* (1971), Robert Barry projected twenty-one slides with short phrases such as "It is purposeful" or "It is influenced." Did these describe art in general or the artwork with its particular adjectives and the order of the slides? Perhaps, but the viewer could just as easily relate them to personal matters, such as their own emotions or relationships. All of this self-referential art recognized that the artist's point of view was not important because viewers actively create their own meanings.

Roland Barthes was a key Structuralist.

15

INVESTIGATION 8, PROPOSITION 2

JOSEPH KOSUTH, 1970

Kosuth believed that avoiding traditional art forms "provided the possibility of seeing how art acquires meaning." In this art installation, each clock is set differently, challenging ideas of recording time. As in many of his works, the books contain writings on various philosophies. Kosuth often quoted philosopher Ludwig Wittgenstein (1889–1951), who had argued in 1921 that every sentence is a picture of the fact that it represents. Wittgenstein later rejected this idea.

INVISIBLE ART

Conceptualism had made the *idea* of art more important than the physical artwork. The next logical step was to get rid of the art object altogether. For some critics, invisible art was a case of "The Emperor's New Clothes." Was the artist tying to trick the viewer? New York artist Robert Barry once said that "Nothing seems to me the most potent thing in the world." Invisible art could also be an effective way to suggest that there is no meaning to life.

For Placid Civil Monument *(1967), American artist Claes Oldenburg hired grave diggers to dig and refill a grave. This invisible art was a protest about the Vietnam War (1955–1975). It implied that the sacrifice of soldiers would also ultimately disappear without a trace.*

MERDA D'ARTISTA
PIERO MANZONI, 1961

The Italian Piero Manzoni (1933–1963) was one of the first artists to play with the idea of invisible art. In 1959, he started drawing lines on sheets of paper that he rolled up and sealed in boxes. On each box, he wrote the line's length, when it was drawn, and signed his name. Of course, the buyer or viewer could not open the box to check that there really was a line inside; if they did, they would destroy the art! The same was true of Manzoni's limited edition of *Merda d'Artista*, ninety cans that supposedly contained his own excrement. The most important aspect of the artwork is the *idea* that the can contains his excrement and what it says about the act of creating and selling art.

16

For his exhibition "White Light/White Heat" (1975), American Chris Burden (b. 1946) lay on a high shelf, hidden from view. The gallery was empty! Part of the experience was deciding if you believed the artist was there.

THROWING IT ALL AWAY

French artist Yves Klein (1928–1962) was obsessed by emptiness, which he called *Le Vide* ("the void"). In 1959, he began selling *Zones of Immaterial Pictorial Sensibility,* which means art that never existed. Buyers were given a *Receipt for the Immaterial,* which they had to burn, destroying any evidence that they "owned" the "art." Klein was paid in thin sheets of gold called gold leaf. In 1962, he scattered half the gold into the Seine River, recording it in photographs. With all these efforts, Klein made his "immaterial" non-art become physical — both in the ideas and rituals used in carrying out the project and in photos.

DOCUMENTING THE INVISIBLE

This creates an interesting problem. Is the art truly invisible if there is a photo that records the event or even a written description of it? The American Robert Barry was one of the most extreme Conceptualists. He was famous for taking photos of transparent gases being released into the air or of transparent threads strung between trees, none of which could be seen. The "invisible" art remained invisible, even to the camera!

NOTHING MATTERS

Barry's weirdest work was *Telepathic Piece* (1969). He wrote in the exhibition catalogue, "During the exhibition, I will try to communicate telepathically a work of art, the nature of which is a series of thoughts that are not applicable to language or image."

HOT AIR?

In 1919, Marcel Duchamp displayed his *L'Air de Paris*, a glass vessel that he had broken open and then resealed. The vessel is a beautiful object, but the idea is the most important part of the piece. Piero Manzoni sold boxes of "artist's breath" that contained a balloon and a stand. People bought the balloons as they were or inflated by the artist; eventually they would deflate anyway.

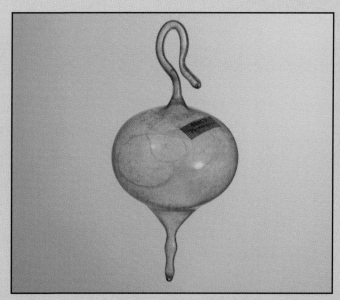

L'AIR DE PARIS, *Marcel Duchamp, 1919*

ART'S HAPPENING

The Conceptual artists were asking many questions: "What is art?" "What form should art take?" During the 1960s and 1970s, the distinction between art and theater blurred. Performance as art sprang up every-where, in hippie happenings (events designed to provoke a response) and at festivals.

THE WEIRD WORLD OF FLUXUS

Originating in Germany, Fluxus was an international art movement of the early 1960s that revived the spirit of Dada. Fluxus Festivals were held across Europe and in New York, with strange performances by artists, musicians, and dancers. Fluxus artists included Germans Joseph Beuys (1921–1986) and Wolf Vostell (1932–1998), Frenchman Robert Filliou (1926–1987), and Americans George Maciunas(1931–1978), Dick Higgins (1938–1998), Nam June Paik (*b.* 1932), and Yoko Ono (*b.* 1933). One of Beuys's performances was *How to Explain Pictures to a Dead Hare* (1965). He smeared his face with honey and gold leaf, walked around holding a dead hare, and explained pictures to it.

Typically, Performance Art was chaotic or absurd. In 1962, Nam June Paik performed his One for Violin Solo, *where he smashed a violin to bits. He thought better quality violins produced better destruction sounds!*

18

Japanese-born American Yoko Ono was a famous performance artist before her marriage to Beatle John Lennon brought her international fame. For their honeymoon in March 1969 (right), they staged a "love-in." At this happening, they made a plea for peace.

THE SINGING SCULPTURE
GILBERT & GEORGE, 1970

When Italian-born Gilbert Proesch (b. 1943) and Britain's George Passmore (b. 1942) first met in 1967, they decided to make their whole lives one long piece of art. They became Gilbert & George and have lived and worked together ever since. Their early pieces were "living sculptures." For *The Singing Sculpture*, they stood on a table and sang "Underneath the Arches" together for eight hours! After 1977, their work focused on "photo-pieces," giant panels of brightly tinted, black-and-white prints of themselves.

STUDENT UPRISINGS

During the 1960s, young people and others believed that demonstrations could change their world. The protest in Paris in 1968 (which Wolf Vostell called "the greatest Happening of all") grew into a national crisis and led to an overhaul of French education. In 1969, Germany's Dusseldorf Academy briefly closed after a rebellion led by artist and professor Joseph Beuys.

Riot police (right) on the streets of Paris in May 1968

ANTI-ART

Fluxus wanted to release people from their inhibitions and to "purge the world of dead art . . . to promote living art, anti-art." Other performance artists shared this goal. To free people to experience art more fully, many performances deliberately provoked viewers' emotions and challenged their assumptions about art.

ART WITH A MESSAGE

Beuys said that politics was "social sculpture." Like many Fluxus artists, he hoped to promote political change. Common issues included sexual freedom, anticapitalism, and equality for women. In their work, Gilbert & George confront prejudices about homosexuality by openly presenting themselves as a gay couple. They explain, "Our reason for making pictures is to change people and not to congratulate them on being how they are."

19

LAND ART

The hippies headed back to nature to escape the artificial environment of cities. In the same spirit, a new type of sculpture emerged, as artists returned to the natural landscape and began making artwork from fields and hills. This movement was called Land Art.

ROLLING STONES

Land artists include Robert Smithson (1938–1973) and James Turrell (*b.* 1943) in the United States and Richard Long (*b.* 1945) and Andy Goldsworthy (*b.* 1956) in Britain. Smithson's *Spiral Jetty* (1970) was a spiral of rocks projecting into Great Salt Lake, Utah. Like much Land Art, its shape was based on nature, and the piece was temporary. After a few years, the lake's level rose and covered it. Some of Long's pieces were just lines of flattened grass where he had walked.

IT'S A WRAP!

Bulgarian-born Christo (*b.* 1935) and his Moroccan-born wife Jeanne-Claude (*b.* 1935) create unique environmental works. Some of it, called *empaquetage*, involves wrapping things up. They raise the money for each project by selling plans and drawings. They don't accept grants or donations. They want to keep their art pure.

Zen rock garden, Japan

SPIRITUALITY IN THE GARDEN
Monks in Japan have raised the garden to an art form, creating "dry landscapes" to promote calm and peace. Zen gardens feature groups of rocks, with each one carefully positioned in gravel. The gravel is raked daily to create fluid ripples. The act of raking is a form of meditation, which can lead to enlightenment, a state of supreme understanding that all Buddhists strive to reach.

Prehistoric stone circles, like Stonehenge (below), *often inspire Land Artists with their spiritual qualities.*

RUNNING FENCE
CHRISTO AND JEANNE-CLAUDE, 1976

Christo and Jeanne-Claude create new environments by introducing new elements. They believe this helps people to view things with new eyes. They like to work in fabric, Christo explains, because it allows people to see "things that cannot usually be seen, like the wind blowing, or the Sun reflecting in ways it had not before." For two weeks in September 1976, their 18-foot- (5.5-meter-) high curtain of white nylon stretched for 25 miles (40 kilometers) across California. It took the couple three-and-a-half years of planning and eighteen public hearings to get their huge project approved and made.

In urban environments, they have wrapped whole buildings and a bridge, the Pont Neuf in Paris (1975–1985).

21

One of the Christos' most ambitious projects was Surrounded Islands *(1983), off the coast of Florida. They surrounded eleven islands with floating rafts of deep pink fabric. Seen from the air, the cloth looked like ballerinas' tutus. Unrolling more than 6.5 million square feet (600,000 square meters) of fabric took a lot of organization. Christo (right) zoomed around in a speedboat, shouting directions.*

LESS IS MORE

To its critics, Minimalist Art seems to show nothing much at all. This art movement arose in the 1950s and has flourished to the present day. Its subject matter is completely pared down so the viewer is free from any distraction. Minimalism focuses on space, form, and physical presence. Like Land Art, it allows the viewer to view the world with fresh eyes and explore what beauty — and art — is all about.

The BEATLES

The cover for the Beatles' White album (1968) was pure white. In contrast to the record covers of the day, it appeared simple, crisp, and clean.

SCULPTURAL SPECIALTIES

The three key Minimalist sculptors are the Americans Donald Judd (1928–1994), Dan Flavin (1933–1996), and Carl Andre (*b.* 1935). All three have specialized in one particular shape or form, repeatedly using it in different works. Judd, for example, is known for his ladders of boxes mounted on a wall. A typical work by Flavin is a bare neon tube placed at an angle. Andre's floor pieces are arrangements of identical or contrasting tiles or blocks.

EQUIVALENT VIII
CARL ANDRE, 1966

Though Andre's eight *Equivalent* sculptures are made of building bricks, the inspiration came from nature while he was canoeing. Andre arranged the bricks in a low, horizontal pattern, like water on a lake. It can be difficult to see what makes a pile of bricks art. When the Tate Gallery in London bought this piece in 1976, many people objected. Andre wanted to alter the viewer's sense of space. Some of his other pieces are even designed to be walked on, to really change the way the viewer relates to the gallery space that a piece is in.

American sculptor Carl Andre (right)

Atheneum's visitor center, designed by Richard Meier

TURNING STAIRS INSIDE OUT

For the Atheneum's visitor center (1979) in Indiana, architect Richard Meier (*b.* 1934) used pure white walls. Their simple curves and lines allowed him to put elements that are usually inside, such as stairs and walks, outside. He highlighted these elements' form without making the entire building seem too cluttered.

SINGLE-COLOR STUDIES

Minimalism also appealed to painters, such as the Americans Frank Stella (*b.* 1936), Ad Reinhardt (1913–1967), and Robert Ryman (*b.* 1930). From the late 1950s until his death, Reinhardt painted a series of all-black works with faint patterns in different shades of black. These works influenced Ryman, who paints only white squares. Despite — or maybe because of — these restrictions, Ryman has been hugely adventurous. He has experimented with white oil paint, acrylic, emulsion, enamel, and pastels. As well as painting on canvas, he has worked with wood, plexiglass, and steel. He is extremely sensitive to how the smallest variation, such as the thickness of a brush stroke, can transform a painting.

23

REALLY REAL

In the late 1960s, a new style of art appeared in the United States, partly born out of Pop and the reaction against Abstract Expressionism. Called Photo-, Hyper, or Superrealism, it presented ordinary people with warts-and-all reality.

CLOSE-UP CANVASES

American artist Chuck Close (*b*. 1940), the greatest of the Photo-Realist painters, always fought against being labeled. In 1997, he explained, "I stayed out of all those Realist shows. I refused to participate not because I hated all that work but because I just wanted to be seen as an individual." Close's first colossal painting from a passport-style photo was *Self-Portrait* (1968). He is still making his heads today by drawing a grid onto a photograph of the subject, then transferring the image, square by square, to a giant canvas.

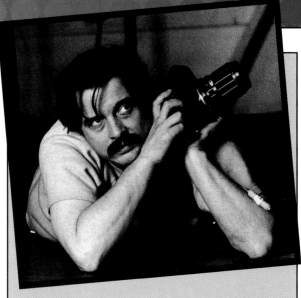

Fashion photographer David Bailey hard at work with his trusty camera

CAUGHT ON CAMERA

British photographer David Bailey (*b*. 1938) exploded onto the 1960s fashion scene. He produced realistic, natural-looking studies of his models. He captured all the popular icons of the decade — actors Michael Caine and Catherine Deneuve, model Jean Shrimpton, and pop stars Marianne Faithfull and Mick Jagger. Bailey was so influential that he became an icon himself. He inspired director Michelangelo Antonioni to make the thriller *Blow-Up* (1966) about a young photographer in swinging London.

HORRIBLE HANSON

The major Superrealist sculptor was American Duane Hanson (1925–1996), who made sculptures of ordinary, everyday people in polyester resin or fiberglass. His approach is so realistic that the images are highly unflattering. Hanson explained, "To me, the resignation, emptiness and loneliness of their existence captures the true reality of life for these people."

YOUNG WOMAN SHOPPER, *Duane Hanson, 1973*

Hanson dressed his figures in real clothes and accessories, such as glasses and shopping bags. The characters always seem to be struggling.

24

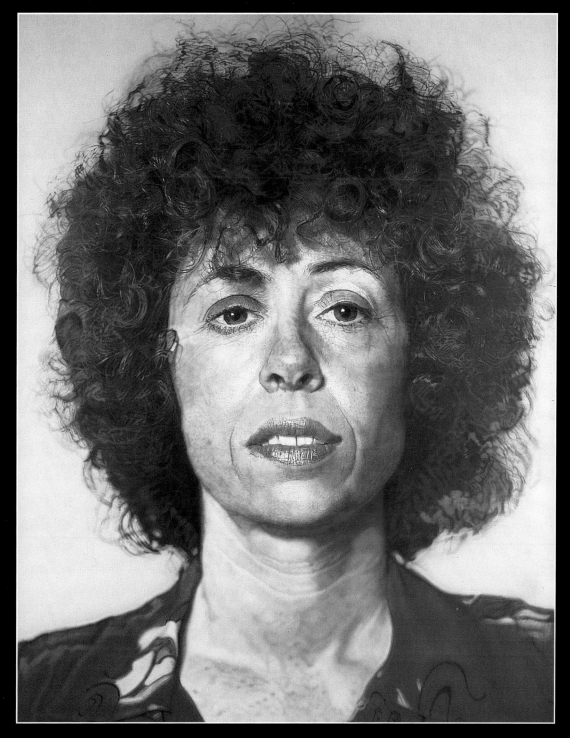

LINDA
CHUCK CLOSE, 1975–1976

Close's works are all titled by the first names of the sitters, and they all dwarf the viewer. This canvas is nearly 9 feet (3 meters) high! Not all are paintings; he also used thumbprints and collages of paper pulp for his portraits. Whatever the method, from a distance, they look just like photographs.

Faithful to the original photo, Close paints only some parts in focus. *Linda*'s face is so sharp that the viewer can see the creases on her skin and even her veins, but at the edges, her hair appears fuzzy. Close said that he wanted to make his works "impersonal and personal, arm's-length and intimate."

AUSTRALIAN ART

Australian Aborigines have been making art for about forty thousand years. Their art is sacred, depicting the myths and beliefs that connect them to their land and their ancestors. As Europeans colonized their country in the 19th century, they forced the Aborigines from their ancient lands. Their art came to show a dialogue between the old myths and their feelings of separation from them.

Body painting (above) *uses earthy colors and sacred themes.*

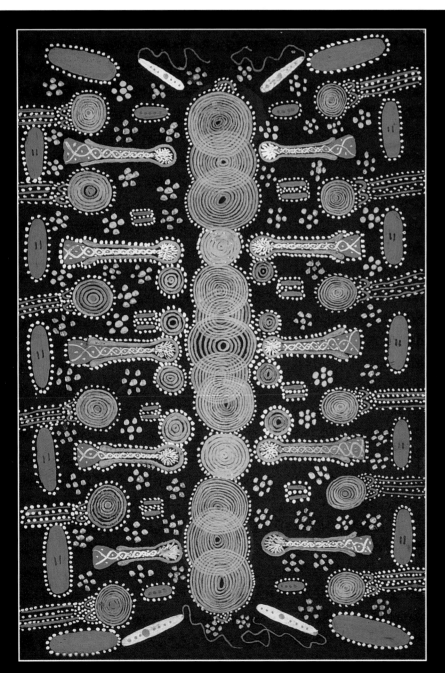

26

MEN'S DREAMING
TIM LEURA TJAPALTJARRI, 1971

Tim Leura Tjapaltjarri (1939–1984) and his brother Clifford Possum Tjapaltjarri (*b. ca* 1932) were two of the first Aboriginal artists to experiment with traditional-style paintings for the international art market. In the 1970s, they moved to Panunya and became part of the Panunya Tula Artists. The brothers worked together on *Warlugulong* (1976), the finest Aboriginal work of the 1970s. Each line, circle, and dot has several different levels of meaning; understanding them requires knowing Aboriginal myths. Artists never reveal the meaning, but non-Aborigines appreciate the style anyway for its beautiful geometric abstraction.

Since the 1960s, Aborigines have fought hard for equal rights. They were not included in Australia's national census until 1967, which meant they were not considered full citizens. In 1976, the Aboriginal Land Rights Act restored some of their land.

FROM BARK TO BOARD

Traditionally, Aboriginal artists painted on rocks and eucalyptus bark, using natural pigments. In the 1970s, Geoffrey Bardon, a schoolteacher at the Panunya settlement, changed that. Bardon wanted the children to learn about their culture's art so he asked elders from Panunya to paint on the school walls. When their mural *Honey Ant Dreaming* (1971) was finished, the elders went on, painting on boards, old doors, and even linoleum, using pigments mixed with modern paints. They put 620 pieces on sale to raise money for more materials, including canvases. Before long, their work had a huge international following.

SACRED MOUNTAIN

Uluru (also known as Ayer's Rock) is a massive outcrop of rock in Western Australia. It holds special significance in Aboriginal myths, but the government did not return it to the Aborigines until 1985. Uluru changes color through the day, over a rich spectrum of reds and browns. Aborigines employ these colors in their art and often use ocher, a natural pigment from the iron-rich earth.

Uluru rises to 1,140 feet (348 meters) and stretches for 2.25 miles (3.6 kilometers).

MAPPING MYTH

The Dreaming is at the heart of Aboriginal culture. Traditional Dreaming stories tell of the Ancestors, magical half-human beings, who walked the land and made it good for humans. These stories can be told with pictures, and some Aboriginal art is best seen as a map. The artists work with their pieces flat on the ground, and the art can be viewed from any angle.

Many Aborigines were forced into government settlements, but some moved to outstations. These communities were on their own land. This outstation in Northern Territory was photographed in 1978.

LATIN AMERICAN ART

In the 1960s and 1970s, South American artists were working in wide-ranging styles. No single movement dominated art as Muralism had during the 1920s and 1930s. Many artists left their country and went to Europe and the United States, either to study for a few years or to settle for good.

INTERNATIONAL STYLE

Venezuelans Jésus Rafael Soto (*b.* 1923) and Carlos Cruz-Diez (*b.* 1923), based in Paris, made Kinetic Art. Soto is famous for his "vibration sculptures," constructions of hanging wires designed to be moved by the viewer.

THE BRILLIANCE OF BOTERO

The most famous of these immigrants is Colombian artist Fernando Botero (*b.* 1932), who has lived in New York and Paris. Botero's paintings are very distinctive — and people either love them or hate them. They all feature strange characters that look like they've been blown up with a bicycle pump! Botero's painting style is rich and lavish, and his work brings high prices.

This cheery papier-maché sculpture is typical of those made to celebrate the Day of the Dead on November 2. Skeletons are used to decorate the tombs of dead relatives.

U.S. president John Kennedy

AFTER VELÁZQUEZ: MARGUERITA
FERNANDO BOTERO, 1977

Botero started to paint his fat figures in the early 1960s. Many are reworkings of famous paintings by Michelangelo da Caravaggio (1571–1610), Diego Velázquez (1599–1660), or Francisco Goya (1746–1828). These artists belong to the times of the Spanish conquistadores and the colonial powers that succeeded them. Many of Botero's fellow artists rejected everything that was Spanish on political grounds, but not him. Instead, he reclaims and transforms the richness of his Spanish heritage, making it his own. "Whether they appear fat or not does not interest me," he said. "It has hardly any meaning for my painting. My concern is with formal fullness, abundance."

CUBAN MISSILE CRISIS

Cuba achieved independence from the old colonial powers after World War II. However, the USSR and the United States then competed to dominate the area. In 1962, Cuban president Fidel Castro allowed the USSR to place nuclear missiles in Cuba, just 90 miles (145 km) from Florida. All over the world, people feared a nuclear war would result, until the USSR eventually agreed to remove the missiles.

MEXICO AFTER MURALISM

In Mexico, art was struggling to be truly Mexican without repeating the heroic, Aztec-style murals of Diego Rivera (1886–1957). Many artists looked to Rufino Tamayo (1899–1991), who drew heavily from folk art and whose parents were Zapotec Indians. Tamayo used deep, rich colors in thick layers of paint. He continued to produce powerful pieces late in life; *Mascara Rojo* (1977) depicts a tortured figure that reminds the viewer of a Day of the Dead skeleton. Tamayo was the major influence on Francisco Toledo (*b.* 1940). Toledo's *The Lazy Dog* (1972) features primitive outlines and thick textures.

LAS MENINAS,
Diego Velázquez, 1656

When Philip IV of Spain made him court painter, Velázquez was just twenty-four. Las Meninas (The Maids of Honor) (below) was one of the artist's last paintings. It shows Philip's daughter, Princess Marguerita. Velázquez lovingly detailed fabrics in his paintings, which Botero also does.

	ART	WORLD EVENTS	DESIGN	THEATER & FILM	BOOKS & MUSIC
1960	•*Klein: IKB 79* •*Tinguely:* Homage to New York	•*Leonid Brezhnev becomes leader of USSR*	•*Grange: Kenwood Chef food mixer*	•Hitchcock's Psycho •Fellini's La Dolce Vita	•*Young:* Poem for Tables, Chairs, Benches
1961	•*Oldenburg: "The Store"* •*Manzoni:* Merda d'Artista	•*Yuri Gagarin in space* •*Berlin Wall built*	•*Saarinen's TWA Terminal at Idlewild (JFK) Airport*	•Broadway: West Side Story •Peter Hall forms the RSC	•*Heller:* Catch-22 •*Grass:* The Tin Drum
1962	•*Warhol:* Marilyn Diptych	•*Cuban Missile Crisis* •*Algerian independence*	•*Giacomo and Castiglioni: Arco lamp*	•*David Lean's* Lawrence of Arabia	•*Burgess:* A Clockwork Orange
1963	•*Lichtenstein:* Whaam! •*Soto:* Horizontal Movement	•*U.S.: President Kennedy assassinated*	•*Gropius and Belluschi's Pan-Am Building, NY*	•*Peter Sellers stars as Dr. Strangelove*	•*Beach Boys:* "Surfin' USA"
1964	•*Bridget Riley:* Current •*Warhol:* Empire State	•*Vietnam War begins* •*S. Africa: Mandela jailed*	•*Japan: Kenzo Tange's Olympic Sports Halls*	•*Andrews as Mary Poppins* •*Harrison in* My Fair Lady	•*The Kinks:* "You Really Got Me"
1965	•*Beuys:* Explaining Paintings to a Dead Hare	•*UK: end of capital punishment*	•*Aarnio:* Globe Chair •*YSL: Mondrian dress*	•*Godard:* Alphaville •Sound of Music	•*Sonny and Cher:* "I Got You, Babe"
1966	•*Carl Andre:* Lever	•*China: Cultural Revolution begins*	•*Saroglia designs the wool trademark symbol*	•*Taylor and Burton:* Who's Afraid of Virginia Woolf?	•*Capote:* In Cold Blood •*Dylan:* Blonde on Blonde
1967	•*Gilbert and George meet* •*Warhol:* Marilyn	•*Six-Day War between Arabs and Israelis*	•*Canada: Moshe Safdie's Habitat Housing*	•*Hippie musical* Hair •*Le Grand Meaulnes*	•*Warhol producer of* The Velvet Underground
1968	•*U.S.A.: Earthworks exhibition*	•*Paris: student riots* •*Aswan Dam completed*	•*U.S.: Lake Point Tower, a glass apartment block*	•2001: A Space Odyssey •Planet of the Apes	•*The Beatles:* White Album •*Hendrix:* Electric Ladyland
1969	•*Kosuth writes "Art after Philosophy" article*	•*Neil Armstrong is the first man on the Moon*	•*Kawakubo founds Comme des Garçons*	•*Orton:* What the Butler Saw •*Fonda:* Easy Rider	•*Georges Perec:* A Void •*Woodstock Music Festival*
1970	•*Hanson:* Tourists •*Smithson:* Spiral Jetty	•*PLO hijacks four planes* •*U.S. troops in Cambodia*	•*Max's Love poster* •*De Pas:* Joe Chair	•*Aboriginal culture hits the big screen with* Walkabout	•*Greer:* The Female Eunuch •*Jackson 5:* ABC
1971	•*Richter:* Brigitte Polk •*Long:* Connemara, Ireland	•*Uganda: Amin in power* •*Greenpeace founded*	•*Piano and Rogers: Pompidou Centre, Paris*	•*Lloyd Webber and Rice's* Jesus Christ Superstar	•*The Doors:* "L.A. Woman" •*Updike:* Rabbit Redux
1972	•*Ellsworth Kelly:* Yellow Red Curve I	•*U.S. troops leave Vietnam* •*Direct rule in Ulster*	•*Switzerland: Botta's Bianchi House*	•*Brando in* The Godfather •*Tarkovsky's* Solaris	•*Italo Calvino:* Invisible Cities •*Moog synthesizer patented*
1973	•*Chuck Close:* Leslie	•*Chile: Pinochet in power* •*Yom Kippur War; oil crisis*	•*Utzon's Sydney Opera House completed*	•*Luis Buñuel:* The Discreet Charm of the Bourgeoisie	•*Thomas Pynchon:* Gravity's Rainbow
1974	•*Botero: Alof de Wignacourt (after Caravaggio)*	•*U.S.: Watergate scandal* •*Turkey invades Cyprus*	•*Des-in studio: Tire sofa*	•*Jack Nicholson stars in* Chinatown	•*ABBA:* "Waterloo" •*Barry Manilow:* "Mandy"
1975	•*Burden:* White Light/ White Heat •*Cragg:* Stack	•*Cambodia overrun by Pol Pot's Khmer Rouge*	•*Britain: Lasdun's National Theatre*	•*Spielberg's* Jaws •Monty Python and the Holy Grail	•*Eno:* Another Green World •*Rushdie:* Grimus
1976	•*Christo and Jeanne-Claude:* Running Fence	•*Viking landers on Mars* •*Aboriginal Land Rights Act*	•*Kenneth Grange styles high-speed 125 train*	•*Stallone:* Rocky •*Bowie in* The Man Who Fell to Earth	•*Glass and Wilson:* Einstein on the Beach
1977	•*Rufino Tamayo:* Mascara Rojo	•*UN bans arms sales to South Africa*	•*Milton Glaser's "I ♥ NY" logo*	•*George Lucas:* Star Wars •Saturday Night Fever	•*Sex Pistols:* God Save the Queen
1978	•*U.S.: Bad Painting exhibition*	•*Vatican: election of Pope John Paul II*	•*U.K.: Foster's Sainsbury Centre for Visual Arts*	•*Parker:* Midnight Express •*Pinter:* Betrayal	•*Hockney designs set for the opera* The Magic Flute
1979	•*Judy Chicago: The Dinner Party*	•*U.K.: Thatcher becomes PM* •*Iran: fall of the Shah*	•*Sony Walkman invented*	•*Ridley Scott:* Alien •*Coppola:* Apocalypse Now	•*Kundera:* The Book of Laughter and Forgetting

30

GLOSSARY

abstraction: the expression of meaning and emotions through shapes and colors.

Abstract Expressionism: a mid-20th-century art movement with a variety of styles and techniques that reflected the artistic freedom to express attitudes and emotion in nontraditional ways.

anticapitalism: against capitalism, an economic system in which individuals own property, farms, and factories and the price of products is determined by competition among the producers.

avant-garde: people who develop new, bold, or experimental concepts, especially in the arts.

collage: an artwork consisting of various materials glued onto a surface.

composition: the way the elements of a work of art make a satisfactory whole.

Constructivism: an art movement based on the belief that artists should create objects society can use, such as furniture.

consumer culture: the customs, beliefs, and way of living that focus extensively on the value of buying and owning objects.

Dada: a movement in art and literature that rejected traditional values and emphasized the absurd.

form: the individual shapes in a work of art and the relationships between them.

self-referential: describing artwork that relies on the viewer to create meaning.

silk-screen: a stencil process in which paint is pressed through silk or other fabric to create a design.

telepathy: communicating ideas only through thoughts, without saying any words aloud.

MORE BOOKS TO READ

The 60s: The Plastic Age. 20th Century Design (series). Julia Bigham (Gareth Stevens)

Aboriginal Art of Australia: Exploring Cultural Traditions. Art around the World (series). Carol Finley (Lerner Publications)

The Art of Optical Illusions. Al Seckel (Carlton Books)

Botero. Great Modern Masters (series). Fernando Botero and Jose Maria Faerna, editor (Abradale Press)

Christo and Jeanne-Claude. Basic Art (series). Jacob Baal-Teshuva, Christo, Jeanne-Claude, and Wolfgang Volz, photographer (Taschen America)

Chuck Close, Up Close. Jan Greenberg and Sandra Jordan (DK Publishing)

Dan Flavin: The Architecture of Light. Dan Flavin and J. Fiona Rageb, editor (Harry N. Abrams)

Performance: Live Art Since 1960. Roselee Goldberg (Harry N. Abrams)

Pop Art. Art Revolutions (series). Linda Bolton (Peter Bedrick Books)

Robert Ryman. Robert and Richard Storr (Tate Gallery Publication)

WEB SITES

WebMuseum: Hockney, David. *www.ibiblio.org/wm/paint/auth/hockney/*

Artcyclopedia: Photorealism. *www.artcyclopedia.com/history/photorealism.html*

Alexander Calder. *www.calder.org/SETS_SUB/home/home_intro_con2.html*

Jean Tinguely. *www.tinguely.ch/Tinguely.engl.html*

Due to the dynamic nature of the Internet, some web sites stay current longer than others. To find additional web sites, use a reliable search engine with one or more of the following keywords: *Aboriginal Art, Conceptualism, Kinectic Art, Mexican Muralism, Minimalism, Op Art, Performance Art, Pop Art, Superrealism,* and the names of individual artists.

INDEX